God redeems the reject

Lawson Hanson

Note: Unless otherwise specified, the cited Bible text references are extracts from the KJV (King James Version, circa 1611) with updated, more modern spelling.

Contents

Chapter 1

Reject beginnings

The author was a bit of a *"reject"* for most of his formative life. Not particularly smart in classes at school and not clever enough to make it into university to pursue any further education — at that time.

He was never made to feel like a *"reject"* by his family or his parents who loved him and cared for him in the best ways they could. They treated all three of their children with the same love and care and concern and we respected and loved them greatly in return for that.

The *"reject"* was a dreadful child at school. He would rather daydream than make the effort to work hard at any studies and he was not always well behaved. I do not think he ever achieved serious *"bad boy"* notoriety.

He was always, or at least most often found, in the wrong place at the wrong time — a bit gullible and slow of wit — I expect he was the perfect fall guy.

The *"reject"* did not seem to make a lot of close friends.

The locations where his family lived could have played a factor in this.

Don't get me wrong. They lived in some beautiful places; he remembers a nice bungalow style house on a large country block with pristine river frontage, way down a long country lane, not far (a long walk) from a small town called Appleton, in Oxfordshire, England.

Later they lived on a large houseboat; yes, a *"houseboat"* with permanent moorings beside the river bank on a stretch of the River Thames called *"Fiddler's Island,"* near Oxford, England. Here is an image of that:

This home was reachable by walking for miles out of the town or city suburbs and across a large stretch of the Port Meadow. This was an idyllic place to live, but none of the other school children lived any where nearby.

He is truthful when he says he got educated at Oxford — in his elementary years. He attended St. Barnabas Church of England school not far from the Oxford University Press.

When he was ten years old he and his family migrated to Australia and it wasn't long before they moved to live at the Royal South Australian Yacht Squadron, at Outer Harbour, where his father had started working as the live-in Caretaker of that private yacht club.

This was another idyllic place to live with sun and sand and lots of fresh air. There was water-side frontage and the ocean nearby and a marina full of sailing boats and power boats. They used to get to go out with Dad in rowboats and a small powered lifeboat on race days.

Outer Harbour was a long way from his schools — located at Largs Bay and later at Semaphore. Most of the other school children lived nowhere close to where they did.

These rather remote places of abode could have contributed towards making the process of developing close friendships a little more difficult.

Is this what made him a *"reject?"* Not entirely sure.

On the positive side — these out of the ordinary locations certainly did provide for interesting times of life with fascinating activities that not everyone else they knew got to share.

He was always a bit of a *"loner."* Happy enough with his own company for most of the time. There were moments when he realised that other people operated in different ways.

The *"reject"* never remembers feeling *"alone"* — there was always so much else to do — swimming, rowing, sailing, fishing and more.

Those around him spent a lot of time *"talking"* to each other and they went dancing and played team sports and they seemed to enjoy a lot of partying.

The *"reject"* always found it difficult to strike up a conversation with others and he spent a lot more solitary time than did others.

Solitary time is not all bad. It provides us with a unique opportunity to deeply examine the inside of our own thinking.

The *"reject"* finds it possible to spend hours thinking about almost anything — enthralled in every moment.

Doing this alone means there is less interruption to the process and he gets to concentrate upon all manner of variations to any particular theme.

He's not saying that solitary thinking is any better nor any worse than less solitary time we spend thinking.

There can be some differences in the outcome — although the result is not always equal, either good or bad.

For example, a solitary thinker could take far longer to reach certain conclusions about matters that will impact others.

The *"reject's"* thinking was always less considerate of others than it needed to be.

If we examine a situation from different angles we may well reach the same or similar conclusions as those who have spent time thinking more collectively with the benefit of input and suggestions from others.

There's no guarantee for either approach to thinking.

Look around the world at some of the awful decisions that get made by committees and other more imposing collective groups.

How does anyone condone wars and atrocities and inhumanity on the scale and in the proportions we see across the world these days?

At least the *"reject"* believes that all life is a precious gift from God and he believes in the veracity of God's commandment: *"Thou shalt not kill."*

The consequences for taking such pre-meditated action needs to be commensurate to the loss or damage we inflict on others.

It's best to think long and hard about all that we do. We need to learn to take responsibility for our actions.

If we (humanity) can't figure out how to do what we know is *"right"* compared to what we know is *"wrong"* then we ought to stop doing anything until we figure out how!

If we take a life — we owe a life.

The one life we own — that we can give in return — is our own life.

If the courts of law choose to take leniency and let us keep our life — then we might consider spending the rest of our life trying to make amends in some meaningful way.

If we have any remorse then we could go and volunteer at a Homeless Shelter or at any one of dozens of other human or animal welfare organizations — and work at that with all our might.

Chapter 2

Reject progress

The *"reject"* remembers one year at high school in religious instruction classes when he sat enthralled as he listened to a Bible believing teacher reading stories about the miracles Jesus performed.

It was obvious to the *"reject"* that this dear lady believed every word she was reading to her class of teenage boys — a delightful experience the *"reject"* always enjoyed each week.

The following year, after a change of teacher, when he asked *"Where are the miracles today?"* The explanation was: *"That was something that Jesus did when He walked the earth and it no longer happens today."*

How sad.

The *"reject"* went away dejected and drifted away from anything to do with religion. How soon was his shallow belief swayed away from his immature and tenuous faith?

I'm happy to report that about a decade later he discovered that second teacher had not known the truth.

The *"reject"* scraped his way through the last two years of high school gaining low *"pass"* grades in technical and science subjects before he started his work life.

The *"reject"* gravitated through a series of different areas of work; as a photographic assistant with a small (Port Adelaide) newspaper, as a sales assistant with an electronics shop, as a radio/radar technician (after training) with the RAAF and then worked as an electronics technician.

For more than a decade of his life he was one of those poor individuals who earned a wage and then spent everything he had.

He never saved any part of his income and always over-spent and thereby he was constantly in debt.

One day in his teenage years, soon after he started work his father gave him some sage advice. He said *"If you earn $100 and try to spend $101, you will be most miserable." "If you earn $100 and never spend more than $99, you will always be happy." "Save a little from your wages, each week."*

He did hear that advice. It took him a long time, to put that sound instruction into practise — unfortunate for him to say the least.

After years of failure and despair he figured out that this required him to *always* live within his means.

This meant that sometimes he would need to pull in his belt a bit and refrain from eating out or buying take-away food all the time.

It meant that he would need to dispense with the notion of always buying the latest new gadget. In later years he learned to keep using his old mobile phone for another year or two instead of replacing that as soon as the new model became available!

At first glance, if we are someone for whom the necessity of the new gadget is always too tantalising to refuse, this may seem like a terrible imposition. Take it from me — we do not miss much.

Most of the features we will find on the latest models get blown out of proportion to their real worth and we can have almost as much fun learning how to better use the features we already have!

Now the peace of mind that accompanies this new way of operating — living within our means — is *worth its weight in gold.*

Not needing to worry about how we will be able to make the next payment on our credit card or find the next installment for our personal loan(s) or be able to afford to pay the rent or the mortgage on time *again.*

Of course, we need to budget for and save amounts sufficient to pay for the borrowings we apply for and accept the responsibility to repay in full.

The reduction in stress from these pressures of modern living can help us to enjoy life more fully.

Don't always think about the one or two gadgets we may not be able to afford; think, rather, about the exciting moments in life that we can soon hope to reasonably afford.

Holidays, overseas travels, saving the deposit for a home of our own, . . .

These can take time for us to accomplish. The good part is they are no longer pipe dreams. They begin to fall within our capability.

Taking the time to learn to live within our means, rather than always living beyond them is a bonus — never an imposition.

We do not need to be a millionaire to be happy.

Of course, the *"reject"* has never tried that in person. He has observed there's lots of those who appear most miserable — struggling with bankruptcy; broken marriages; financial ruin; drugs; crime; and the like.

Without ever making that lofty financial grade of wealth the *"reject"* has found a happy space.

The small and simple elements of life can bring far more joy than the flamboyant and the grandiose.

May the Lord bless you as you consider how God redeemed the *"reject."*

Chapter 3

Reject gets a future

Like many of his peers, by the time the *"reject"* reached the age of 25, he was drinking, swearing, dabbling in drugs, smoking about 30 cigarettes every day and if he's honest with himself he was well beyond the definition of a borderline alcoholic.

Soon after his discharge from serving in the RAAF an astonishing turn of events transpired.

Having been out of work for about four or five months, he applied for an advertised position as an Electronics Technician in the Physics Department of the University of Melbourne.

The *"reject"* got selected to attend an interview for this employment and a day or two later he learned that he had missed out by one.

That Friday night there was a big — come one, come all — kind of party at the large house where he was renting a room.

The *"reject"* thinks he smoked something which must have had a residue of an insecticide or other poison because he had an awful reaction to it and began to feel so sick that he thought he was going to die. Rapid heart rate — sweating profusely — difficulty breathing — drifting in and out of consciousness — a great concern to say the least.

At that time he called out to God saying: *"If you are there God, please don't let me die.";* then he fell asleep and remembers nothing until late the next morning. He slept for most of this and the following day.

On the Monday morning there was a ring at the doorbell. The Postman arrived with a telegram addressed to the *"reject!"*

The telegram was from the Department of Civil Engineering at the University of Melbourne and they were offering him a position as an Electronics Technician in their department because they had heard of him from the Department of Physics who it seems had recommended him as a possible candidate for their requirements. He went in for another interview and got offered the position which he was glad to accept.

A week or so after the *"reject"* started to work at their large reinforced floor Structures Laboratory — a Ph.D. student returned from semester break to resume his project work.

From this student the *"reject"* began to hear again about the wonderful miracles of Jesus, and moreover, that there's proof to be had of the existence of God.

God still performs miracles of healing and provision and delivers a great sense of comfort and joy to His people today.

Now the *"reject"* thought he had heard it all before — this was different.

Instead of needing to somehow have a blind faith in a God who would never communicate with us he got told about the *"real"* Almighty God of Creation.

There is one God who can and who will answer us — if we will call to Him.

The Bible book of Jeremiah tells us God says this:

> 3. *Call unto me, and I will answer thee, and shew thee great and mighty things, which thou knowest not.*
> — Jeremiah 33:3

The God described in the Bible is and has always been a miracle working God.

For starters He created the heavens and the earth and all that therein is.

Look at the countryside around you or gaze up into the starry sky at night and consider the grandeur of God's Creation — give Him praise and thanks for all He has done and all He continues to do for us.

The Bible is full of descriptions of God's interactions with men and women who took the time to appreciate Him.

If we look with a little care there are instructions within the pages of the Bible to help us make personal contact with Almighty God.

Consider these words that Jesus spoke to Nicodemus:

> 1. *There was a man of the Pharisees, named Nicodemus, a ruler of the Jews:*
> 2. *The same came to Jesus by night, and said unto him, Rabbi, we know that thou art a teacher come from God: for no man can do these miracles that thou doest, except God be with him.*
> 3. *Jesus answered and said unto him, Verily, verily, I say unto thee, Except a man be born again, he cannot see the kingdom of God.*

4. Nicodemus saith unto him, How can a man be born when he is old? can he enter the second time into his mother's womb, and be born?
5. Jesus answered, Verily, verily, I say unto thee, Except a man be born of water and of the Spirit, he cannot enter into the kingdom of God.
6. That which is born of the flesh is flesh; and that which is born of the Spirit is spirit.
7. Marvel not that I said unto thee, Ye must be born again.
— John 3:1–7

Look at the imperative words that Jesus used: *"Ye must be born again."*

What on earth does *"born again"* mean? How can such an event take place?

At the end of the book of Luke, and at the start of the book of Acts, their author (Luke) reports that, among the last instructions given by Jesus, to His disciples, are these:

49. And, behold, I send the promise of my Father upon you: but tarry ye in the city of Jerusalem, until ye be endued with power from on high.
— Luke 24:49

The word *"tarry"* means they were to *wait* in Jerusalem. Something important was about to occur.

In the first chapter of Acts the word Jesus used got translated as *"wait:"*

4. And, being assembled together with them, commanded them that they should not depart from Jerusalem, but wait for the promise of the Father, which, saith he, ye have heard of me.

14

5. *For John truly baptized with water; but ye shall be baptized with the Holy Ghost not many days hence.*
— Acts 1:4–5

These faithful disciples did as Jesus instructed (*commanded*) and they waited for the *"promise of the Father."*

Chapter two (2) of the book of Acts describes what happened:

1. *And when the day of Pentecost was fully come, they were all with one accord in one place.*
2. *And suddenly there came a sound from heaven as of a rushing mighty wind, and it filled all the house where they were sitting.*
3. *And there appeared unto them cloven tongues like as of fire, and it sat upon each of them.*
4. *And they were all filled with the Holy Ghost, and began to speak with other tongues, as the Spirit gave them utterance.*
— Acts 2:1–4

This is the experience that Jesus called *"born again,"* emphasising the necessity for us to get *"born of the Spirit."*

The Bible account records that a great crowd of people heard a lot of commotion when these initial 120 people received their tangible, audible (speaking in other tongues) baptism with the Holy Ghost.

This crowd began to ask questions:

12. *And they were all amazed, and were in doubt, saying one to another, What meaneth this?*
— Acts 2:12

Peter the disciple of Jesus, stood up and began to explain what was taking place. He expounded parts of their scriptures he knew they would have heard before, for example:

> 16. *But this is that which was spoken by the prophet Joel;*
> 17. *And it shall come to pass in the last days, saith God, I will pour out of my Spirit upon all flesh: and your sons and your daughters shall prophesy, and your young men shall see visions, and your old men shall dream dreams:*
> 18. *And on my servants and on my handmaidens I will pour out in those days of my Spirit; and they shall prophesy:*
> 19. *And I will shew wonders in heaven above, and signs in the earth beneath; blood, and fire, and vapour of smoke:*
> 20. *The sun shall be turned into darkness, and the moon into blood, before the great and notable day of the Lord come:*
> 21. *And it shall come to pass, that whosoever shall call on the name of the Lord shall be saved.*
> — Acts 2:16–21

Peter spoke to them at length and some of what he said prompted somebody in the crowd to ask: "*What shall we do?*"

Peter's response was this:

> 38. *Then Peter said unto them, Repent, and be baptized every one of you in the name of Jesus Christ for the remission of sins, and ye shall receive the gift of the Holy Ghost.*
> 39. *For the promise is unto you, and to your children, and to all that are afar off, even as many as the LORD our God shall call.*

We can read how another three *thousand* people — yes 3,000 people on that same day followed Peter's advice and they also received this personal and mighty reassurance from the Almighty God of all Creation.

What can we do?

Read verse 39 again: *"For the promise is unto you, and to your children, and to all that are afar off, even as many as the LORD our God shall call."*

Even though we could dwell far away (geographically) from that location and we are far away in time — almost 2,000 years — those words tell us: *"the promise is unto you."*

Please don't let this opportunity pass you by.

Peter, now *"filled with the Holy Ghost,"* gave a clear presentation of the solution:

1. Repent
   means to have a change of thinking where necessary; take a step towards God, rather than drifting further away. Do what He asks us to do. He has a purpose for asking us to *"repent."*

2. Be baptized every one of you
   baptism means fully immersed in water and is symbolic of burying or putting away the old *"you"* and getting ready for the new *"born again"* version

3. You will receive the gift of the Holy Ghost
   this is the *"promise of the Father"* that Jesus said God will freely give to those who will make this humble approach and then ask and call on God for His gift

The act of getting *"baptized,"* shows *"the answer of a good conscience toward God,"* as we can read in first Peter, chapter 3, verse 21:

> 21. *The like figure whereunto even baptism doth also now save us (not the putting away of the filth of the flesh, but the answer of a good conscience toward God,) by the resurrection of Jesus Christ*
> — 1 Peter 3:21

Like all those followers, we will also: *"speak with other tongues, as the Spirit gives us the utterance"* when we *"receive the gift of the Holy Ghost."*

We do not need to go to college to learn how to speak a foreign language. This is an instantaneous part of *"the promise of the Father,"* that Jesus had spoken to them about already.

Chapter 4

Today's good news

The "*good news*" is that God is still calling out today — to anyone who will listen to His call.

Repent — prepare to get your thinking changed if needed.

For a moment — at least — we can put aside our old religious teaching and re-examine these words that God has preserved in His Word — the Bible — for us to read — and for us to act on.

We might need to straighten out our lives and actions to help us conform to the way we know God wants us to behave:

> 8. *He hath shewed thee, O man, what is good; and what doth the LORD require of thee, but to do justly, and to love mercy, and to walk humbly with thy God?*
> — Micah 6:8

From the "*reject's*" experience — this does not hurt. Try it.

We can start to feel good about ourself.

Show mercy to others; do not seek revenge. Jesus says we should turn the other cheek, and forgive people who do any wrong to us.

We find they do not know or understand the full extent of the grace and mercy of God.

Preach the gospel to them in a gentle manner. That could help.

We are God's creation; not the other way around.

Don't shout at God. He can hear us.
Don't curse and swear. He will turn away.

We need to approach God in a circumspect manner with heart felt honesty and humility; a state of repentance where we want to find the truth.

Here is the *specified* way to make personal contact with God and have Him provide *spiritual* contact with us, so both we and those around us can know for sure that we have done what's required (*commanded* as being mandatory for us by the words of Jesus): "*You must be born again.*"

How can we get to have this same experience?

It's a three step process:

1. Repent

We turn aside from doing our own thing all the time.

Make a humble and honest approach towards God.

2. Get baptized

Do what God has asked us to do.

Go through the short process of water baptism.

It demonstrates our intentions are good.

It takes a little bit of humility. Yes we'll get wet.

In the church I attend we use warm water.
We have a fresh supply of shorts and tee shirts
and dry towels — for people who don't bring their
own.

The Bible says *"all have sinned and come short of the glory of God."*

Jesus died to wash away our sins.

3. **Receive God's Holy Spirit**

Ask God for the promise of the Father.

Spend time talking to God with humility and sincerity.

Worship God — saying the word *"Hallelujah"* gives praise to God and helps to keep us talking.

We need to be speaking to let God change the words.

Say thank you for what we are expecting to receive.

We will know the moment we receive the *"promise of the Father"* because we will start speaking in an unlearned tongue.

If this takes a little while, do not get discouraged.

Ask and keep on asking. Jesus says:

> 7. *Ask, and it shall be given you; seek, and
> ye shall find; knock, and it shall be opened
> unto you:*
> 8. *For every one that asketh receiveth; and
> he that seeketh findeth; and to him that
> knocketh it shall be opened.*
> — Matthew 7:7–8

The only people who will not receive this free gift from God is one who gives up too soon — or one who is not prepared to do what God asks of us.

Why would we let either of these reasons impede our progress from making personal, tangible, evidential contact with Almighty God?

The *"reject"* is an ordinary — run of the mill person — nothing special.

He gives great praise and thanks to God for redeeming him from the edge of perdition.

If God cares enough to save such a one as me, then He is most certain to have the same care and concern for you.

There's nothing more precious than knowing God — in person.

Chapter 5

God works miracles

The changes this same experience brought about in the life of the *"reject"* is nothing short of miraculous.

It took the *"reject"* about five or six months to accept an invitation to attend a meeting at the church to which his new acquaintance went:

> https://www.revivalcentres.org

The *"reject"* was a bit slow when it came to making decisions about anything new — he was cautious.

Walking through the doors of the Revival Centres Church felt as if he was coming home! It's a happy place with a sea of genuine smiling faces.

If truth be known he wishes he had never dragged his feet for so long before coming along.

These people come from all walks of life and they are happy and content and spend time giving their thanks and appreciation to God for His miracles of healing and blessings in their lives.

The *"reject"* got baptized after his second meeting.

For the first time in over a decade the *"reject"* felt as if he had taken a step in the right direction — towards God instead of always moving the other way.

Five weeks after getting baptized, in the manner that John the Baptist used — by complete immersion in water — the *"reject"* received his own *"day of Pentecost"* experience.

Receiving the gift of the Holy Spirit is wonderful.

He was speaking in other tongues as the Spirit gave him the utterance. His speech was quiet, yet clear.

This audible gift gives us a personal prayer language that gets used for our direct communication with Almighty God.

It's a precious gift that He expects us to use every day.

It brings great benefits including peace and comfort and joy. It provides Spiritual insight into the kingdom of God.

Look at these added benefits. This list of *"fruit"* of the Spirit is part of the composite gift that God provides to us:

> 22. *But the fruit of the Spirit is love, joy, peace, longsuffering, gentleness, goodness, faith,*
> 23. *Meekness, temperance: against such there is no law.*
> — Galatians 5:22–23

These expressions of God's Holy Spirit become a part of our own persona — if we will let them and not hinder His goodness.

We discover the true love of God that brings us endless joy and peace that passes all understanding. We find we can express patience (longsuffering) and display real gentleness and goodness — mild manners and level headedness as we use the perfect measure of faith God gives to each of us:

1. I beseech you therefore, brethren, by the mercies of God, that ye present your bodies a living sacrifice, holy, acceptable unto God, which is your reasonable service.
2. And be not conformed to this world: but be ye transformed by the renewing of your mind, that ye may prove what is that good, and acceptable, and perfect, will of God.
3. For I say, through the grace given unto me, to every man that is among you, not to think of himself more highly than he ought to think; but to think soberly, according as God hath dealt to every man the measure of faith.
— Romans 12:1–3

Instead of getting upset and bothered and angry we can express meekness and temperance because we know that God is on our side and we will not fail — if we will look to Him for help.

God will bless what we attempt to do — provided those undertakings are true and honest and upright in His sight.

Don't expect God to bless any underhanded activity that we know is wrong and unfair or unjust.

In a split second, on the 27th July, 1975, the *"reject"* knew for certain that God is real and that God loves him more than he can imagine.

There's One God who *can* answer our call. He promises He will.

Almighty God is God of all Creation. He and His Son, Jesus Christ, have provided a way for us to receive the gift of the Holy Spirit. This provides us with our own evidence of the absolute veracity of God and His Word.

During the five weeks interval between when the *"reject"* got baptized, on Sunday the 22nd June, 1975, and then after taking that action, he received the gift of the Holy Spirit, on Sunday 27th July, 1975, he experienced his own remarkable, *personal* miracles from God.

One evening he attended a smaller, mid-week, *"house meeting"* where all he remembers hearing is: *"God is a healing God."*

Near the end of that meeting, during a brief time of prayer, he raised his hand to get one of the leaders to pray for him.

He asked for prayer that God would heal his nose. It had been in pain for about one whole year after he got punched in the face during a bit of a fight.

The person who prayed for him said these simple words: *"Thank you God for healing this man's nose"* followed by a couple of statements like: *"Hallelujah, praise the Lord,"* *"Hallelujah"* and *"Bless Your wonderful Name"* and a final *"Thank You Jesus."*

Simple words of prayer and honest giving of thanks to God. Soon after that the *"reject"* went home.

During the night the *"reject"* woke up feeling rather warm and there was a tingling sensation in the middle of his face. It felt as if his nose was getting manipulated around and around in a gentle and tiny circular motion.

He got up to check there was nobody else there. He lived alone.

In the middle of winter in Melbourne, he soon cooled down. Then he went back to bed and slept soundly.

In the morning there was another new sensation: No more pain!

Wow. Healed over night. Thank you Lord.

At another small house meeting in the next week or two he heard the powerful statement: *"God can do anything!"*

He took it upon himself to say to God: *"Okay God. If you can do anything?"* *"Stop me from smoking."* Almost a challenge. He does not think he even remembered to say: *"Please."* Sorry Lord.

Later that night, after he got home from the meeting, he went to light up a cigarette before heading off to bed. At that time he was already a chain smoker — over 30 each day.

That cigarette tasted awful; horrible; foul. In despair, he opened a new carton of cigarettes, took out a fresh pack and tried to light up another cigarette, discovering that the *new* one tasted awful, too.

In disbelief (almost) he went to bed and slept soundly until the next morning. When he awoke he tried to light up another cigarette. It tasted disgusting!

Then he realised that God enabled him to quit smoking — *overnight.*

All his praises go to God.

If you have ever been a smoker you will understand how difficult is the act of giving up that addiction to nicotine. He had at previous times tried quitting by himself and had always failed within a day or two at most.

Since that day (over 50 years ago now) he has never had the craving for another cigarette; in fact even the slightest smell of cigarette smoke makes him feel ill. It always serves as a good reminder about this miracle God performed for the *"reject"* — even *before* he was *"born again."*

One day during those first five weeks the desire to drink alcohol deserted him. In truth, he was an alcoholic — taking strong drink almost every day — always unable to refrain. Another reason why his spending was out of control.

He had the sudden urge to pour his small collection of beer

and wines and spirits down the sink. He lined up the bottles and he did. It felt most *liberating.*

Since doing that he has never wanted to touch another glass of beer or wine or alcohol of any kind.

He noticed another miracle: his speech was beginning to contain less and less profanities and expletives. He could almost string together a couple of sentences without the need for any of those vulgar, objectionable terms.

Expletives — rude words are meaningless noise. Leave them out.

Thrilled by the fact that his senses of taste and smell were starting to return this soon after he had stopped smoking and drinking the *"reject"* got delighted by these personal miracles.

The next time he tasted a fresh ripe tomato his taste buds exploded with the sensations of this flavour he had not properly tasted since he was a youth.

The rejuvenation of the *"reject's"* taste buds was nothing short of miraculous.

These miracles coupled with the realisation that he was sleeping soundly *every* night instead of tossing and turning half awake for hours on end as he had been before — gave him great reason the give thanks to God.

He was at home, praying by himself saying words like: *"Hallelujah"* and small phrases like: *"Praise the Lord"* and *"Thank you Lord."* In his mind he was asking God for the promise of the Father, the Holy Spirit.

He was thanking the Lord as he was thinking about those remarkable miracles of healing and provision that God had *already* performed for the *"reject."*

After a short space of time, while giving God thanks and

repeating those two or three words of prayer he had learned, the *"reject"* realised he had actually received the gift of the Holy Spirit.

How did he know? He was speaking in other tongues. His speech was quiet, yet clear, with an unmistakable change. The words streamed out of his mouth. There was no extraordinary effort required.

He could stop the praying in tongues and he could start praying in tongues again. He was in complete control of this wonderful gift that God had graciously bestowed upon him.

It felt wonderful and he kept praying for a little while longer listening to those unknown words. A scripture he had heard three or four days earlier came to mind:

> 14. *For if I pray in an unknown tongue,*
> *my spirit prayeth, but my understanding is*
> *unfruitful.*
> — 1 Corinthians 14:14

He realised that he was able to do what God wanted:

> 24. *God is a Spirit: and they that worship him*
> *must worship him in spirit and in truth.*
> — John 4:24

He realised that miracles still *do* happen today.

That second high school teacher was speaking without any personal experience – how could he know?

The God of all creation has never changed.

Consider these verses from the book of Malachi:

> 6. *For I am the LORD, I change not; therefore*
> *ye sons of Jacob are not consumed.*

> 7. *Even from the days of your fathers ye are*
> *gone away from mine ordinances, and have not*
> *kept them. Return unto me, and I will return*
> *unto you, saith the LORD of hosts. But ye said,*
> *Wherein shall we return?*
> — Malachi 3:6–7

We don't even realise we have walked so far away from what God wants and expects from us — His beloved creation.

And this verse in the book of Hebrews:

> 8. *Jesus Christ the same yesterday, and to day,*
> *and for ever.*
> — Hebrews 13:8

These verses mean we can take God and Jesus Christ at their word. We can expect the statements they have made to remain true for all time.

Elsewhere the Word of God says this:

> 19. *God is not a man, that he should lie; neither*
> *the son of man, that he should repent: hath he*
> *said, and shall he not do it? or hath he spoken,*
> *and shall he not make it good?*
> — Numbers 23:19

We can trust and rely upon the promises of God.

The author no longer felt like he was the *"reject."*

Almighty God had reached out and answered his call.

There's no rejection in that!

God's promised gift is for everyone, every where.

No longer do we need to get caught up in any of these ways of the world:

19. *Now the works of the flesh are manifest, which are these; Adultery, fornication, uncleanness, lasciviousness,*
20. *Idolatry, witchcraft, hatred, variance, emulations, wrath, strife, seditions, heresies,*
21. *Envyings, murders, drunkenness, revellings, and such like: of the which I tell you before, as I have also told you in time past, that they which do such things shall not inherit the kingdom of God.*
— Galatians 5:19–21

All the more reason to give praise and thanks to God and to His Son Jesus Christ — without Whom we would be forever lost in sin.

Chapter 6

Reject repentance

The first part of the instructions Peter the apostle gave in response to the question *"What shall we do?"* was *"Repent."*

An initial image that may come to mind in respect to the term *"repent,"* is that of being utterly sorrowful for something terrible we have done. You may imagine something like this, described in the book of Job:

> 6. *Wherefore I abhor myself, and repent in dust and ashes.*
> — Job 42:6

We could have made terrible decisions and taken thoughtless action from time to time. We could need to confront such feelings of complete remorse. We are all different.

Other people consider themselves as basically *"good people,"* and find themselves asking *"Why should I repent?"* *"I haven't done anything wrong."*

Perhaps the thing we have done wrong, is that we have turned our back on the God of Creation. This may not have been willfully done. It's because none of our family or close acquaintances believe in God and we do not know the truth about the God of the Bible.

The book of Romans contains this succinct statement about us:

> 23. *For all have sinned, and come short of the glory of God;*
> — Romans 3:23

It explains in more details like the following excerpts:

> 12. *Wherefore, as by one man sin entered into the world, and death by sin; and so death passed upon all men, for that all have sinned:*
> 13. *(For until the law sin was in the world: but sin is not imputed when there is no law.*
> 14. *Nevertheless death reigned from Adam to Moses, even over them that had not sinned after the similitude of Adam's transgression, who is the figure of him that was to come.*
> 15. *But not as the offence, so also is the free gift. For if through the offence of one many be dead, much more the grace of God, and the gift by grace, which is by one man, Jesus Christ, hath abounded unto many.*
> 16. *And not as it was by one that sinned, so is the gift: for the judgment was by one to condemnation, but the free gift is of many offences unto justification.*
> 17. *For if by one man's offence death reigned by one; much more they which receive abundance of grace and of the gift of righteousness shall reign in life by one, Jesus Christ.)*
> 18. *Therefore as by the offence of one judgment came upon all men to condemnation; even so by*

the righteousness of one the free gift came upon
all men unto justification of life.
19. For as by one man's disobedience many were
made sinners, so by the obedience of one shall
many be made righteous.
— Romans 5:12–19

The death of Jesus Christ, and the shedding of his blood, provided the way for our forgiveness. This verse in the book of Colossians says that rather succinctly:

14. In whom we have redemption through his
blood, even the forgiveness of sins:
— Colossians 1:14

The Old Testament declares that God will be merciful to us:

6. Seek ye the LORD while he may be found, call
ye upon him while he is near:
7. Let the wicked forsake his way, and the
unrighteous man his thoughts: and let him return
unto the LORD, and he will have mercy upon
him; and to our God, for he will abundantly
pardon.
— Isaiah 55:6–7

The *"reject"* needed to re-adjust his thinking! He needed to work out what *"repentance"* meant and then what his repentance meant.

We can think of the term *"repent"* (Gk: metanoeo) as meaning another form of thinking that will coexist with our ordinary every-day thinking. It doesn't change our own natural ability to think. It provides us with extra capability to understand points which we may have dismissed before.

Repentance means to be more mindful about how we think; or in other words, we should inspect the evidence and take the recommended actions.

We may not be able to go back in time to that *"day of Pentecost,"* to see what took place there. That does not matter. We can have our own experience of receiving the gift of the Holy Ghost.

We should *"re-think"* our position, and our belief (or lack of belief) in God.

Take an honest, in-depth look at what the Bible says. We need to read with open eyes, with an open mind, and an open heart.

Dare for a moment to believe that this is true! Ask the God of the Bible to illuminate our understanding and to prove Himself to us.

Don't let our old thinking cloud this new found comprehension of the truth of God's Word.

Chapter 7

God given blessings

At our church — between the meetings — most of its members speak to people of all ages and from different walks of life and enjoy the opportunity to do so.

Of course, during the meetings we enjoy listening to the Holy Spirit inspired teaching presented by our pastors and leaders — because these get soundly based on the Bible — and we believe that is the precious Word of God.

About twelve weeks after the *"reject"* had started attending church on a regular basis — another six or seven weeks after the time he received the gift of God's Holy Spirit, a young lady returned after being away during the school holidays — she was a primary school teacher.

That Sunday these two were sitting in the same row of seats. At the end of the meeting after most people had gotten up to converse with others or go for coffee they were both still there.

The *"reject"* was casting a glance around to see if any one he knew was still there. When his eyes rested for a moment on the young lady in the same row of seats his heart melted.

In a moment he thought: *"That's the woman I want to*

marry!"

Love at first sight — not a shred of doubt.

After brief introductions: — *"Hi, I'm Lawson."* — *"Hi, I'm Heather."* — they began to converse with each other.

Over the next weeks they started going out for coffee with others from church and enjoyed each other's company.

During a serious moment the *"reject"* said: *"I think I'm in love with you."* Heather blushed a little then smiled and said: *"Me too."*

From that moment on it was almost a *fait accompli.*

At Christmas time we both went across to Adelaide — allowing me to introduce Heather to my parents. I think they loved her from the moment they met her, too.

We got married at the start of the next year and have almost reached our 50th wedding anniversary.

We both feel most blessed by God's great provision in our lives and we thoroughly identify with these verses in Psalms 37:

> 4. *Delight thyself also in the LORD: and he shall give thee the desires of thine heart.*
> 5. *Commit thy way unto the LORD; trust also in him; and he shall bring it to pass.*
> — Psalms 37:4–5

Unlike us, God has no earthly limitations on His ability. This verse about the boundless grace of God and His ability to do more than we ask or think — always resounds with me:

> 20. *Now unto him that is able to do exceeding abundantly above all that we ask or think, according to the power that worketh in us,*

— Ephesians 3:20

There has been no shortage of God's blessings in our lives.

Before hearing the good news about the *"promise of the Father"* and receiving this wonderful gift from God, the *"reject"* had spent almost a decade working in those other occupations.

Soon the *"reject"* got the opportunity to develop an interest in writing computer software — something he had wanted to do since hearing the word *"computer"* in high school.

He needed to use a bit of software to help him analyse the data he collected from an electronic data-logger he was using in part of his work in the Civil Engineering Structures Laboratory.

Martin, the same person who preached the gospel to the *"reject"* knew how to write programs in the Fortran language — this was ideal. He spent time in his lunch breaks and other spare moments helping the *"reject"* to learn some of the basics of programming in Fortran — most helpful.

The *"reject"* became reasonably productive, even proficient, at one or two aspects of this new skill.

Other work opportunities began to present themselves, for which he gives God great praise.

Long before his working life was over the *"reject"* managed to find productive and intellectually rewarding employment with organisations like: CSIRO, Email-York Ltd., and MPA International P/L, before he next managed to start and run his own computer consulting business for ten (10) years — during which time he worked for other organisations like: Community Services of Victoria, Telecom Australia, BHP Petroleum P/L, Telstra Ltd., IBM-GSA and NEC Australia P/L.

In 2004, after the Y2K work had dried up he went back to work full time for fourteen years with a world class climate research team at the Bureau of Meteorology.

The *"reject"* counts himself most fortunate to have spent the last 40 years of his working life employed in positions that he has thoroughly enjoyed.

The *"reject"* even managed to write computer programs he got to run on world class supercomputers — owned or shared by his employers.

He gives eternal thanks to God for opening doors and for blessing the work of his hands that he undertook to perform.

Chapter 8

Walking On In Faith

Our conduct needs to be beyond reproach.

We get reminded of this in verses like the following excerpt from the book of Titus:

> 1. *Put them in mind to be subject to principalities and powers, to obey magistrates, to be ready to every good work,*
> 2. *To speak evil of no man, to be no brawlers, but gentle, shewing all meekness unto all men.*
> 3. *For we ourselves also were sometimes foolish, disobedient, deceived, serving divers lusts and pleasures, living in malice and envy, hateful, and hating one another.*
> 4. *But after that the kindness and love of God our Saviour toward man appeared,*
> 5. *Not by works of righteousness which we have done, but according to his mercy he saved us, by the washing of regeneration, and renewing of the Holy Ghost;*
> 6. *Which he shed on us abundantly through Jesus Christ our Saviour;*
> 7. *That being justified by his grace, we should be*

made heirs according to the hope of eternal life.
— Titus 3:1–7

Verse three reminds us that before we receive *"the promise of the Father"* — we were sometimes *"foolish and disobedient and deceived"* — living on the wrong side of life.

We give God great praise and thanks because it is *"Not by works of righteousness which we have done."*

Rather — it's because of God's never ending grace and mercy and His kindness and love towards us.

In verse five the terms *"regeneration"* and *"renewing"* — *"of the Holy Ghost"* concur with the advice Jesus gave Nicodemus when he said *"Ye must be born again."*

There's a vast difference between human wisdom and God's wisdom:

> 18. *Let no man deceive himself. If any man among you seemeth to be wise in this world, let him become a fool, that he may be wise.*
> 19. *For the wisdom of this world is foolishness with God. For it is written, He taketh the wise in their own craftiness.*
> 20. *And again, The Lord knoweth the thoughts of the wise, that they are vain.*
> — Colossians 3:18–20

Verse 17 in James chapter 3 tells us about God's wisdom:

> 17. *But the wisdom that is from above is first pure, then peaceable, gentle, and easy to be intreated, full of mercy and good fruits, without partiality, and without hypocrisy.*
> — James 3:17

We need to stay inspired by The Creator and His Word. This means we need to get busy reading and listening to what God has said to us.

> 1. *Blessed is the man that walketh not in the counsel of the ungodly, nor standeth in the way of sinners, nor sitteth in the seat of the scornful.*
> 2. *But his delight is in the law of the LORD; and in his law doth he meditate day and night.*
> 3. *And he shall be like a tree planted by the rivers of water, that bringeth forth his fruit in his season; his leaf also shall not wither; and whatsoever he doeth shall prosper.*
> 4. *The ungodly are not so: but are like the chaff which the wind driveth away.*
> 5. *Therefore the ungodly shall not stand in the judgment, nor sinners in the congregation of the righteous.*
> 6. *For the LORD knoweth the way of the righteous: but the way of the ungodly shall perish.*
> — Psalms 1:1–6

We don't want to be like the ungodly.

Let your *"delight"* get founded *"in the law of the LORD."*

We can carry the entire Word of God — the Bible — wherever we go in an App on our smartphone.

Read some every day. Learn to navigate the search function.

God continues to speak to us through His Word today.

God's Word is fresher than tomorrow's news. It never grows old or outdated.

God knows the end from the beginning:

*9. Remember the former things of old: for I am
God, and there is none else; I am God, and there
is none like me,*
*10. Declaring the end from the beginning, and
from ancient times the things that are not yet
done, saying, My counsel shall stand, and I will
do all my pleasure:*
*11. Calling a ravenous bird from the east, the
man that executeth my counsel from a far
country: yea, I have spoken it, I will also bring
it to pass; I have purposed it, I will also do it.*
— Isaiah 46:9–11

The Word of God contains wonderful promises for His
people. We get to become God's people when He adopts us
into His family:

*13. For if ye live after the flesh, ye shall die: but
if ye through the Spirit do mortify the deeds of
the body, ye shall live.*
*14. For as many as are led by the Spirit of God,
they are the sons of God.*
*15. For ye have not received the spirit of bondage
again to fear; but ye have received the Spirit of
adoption, whereby we cry, Abba, Father.*
— Romans 8:13–15

What a privileged position.

Chapter 9

Giving glory to God

God can do anything — including lifting you up and turning you around and setting you on a new and more righteous trajectory.

We need to decide that is where we want to be.

We need to stop thinking we know better than God. That's an impossibility.

We need to exercise humility and acknowledge that God — The Creator — knows far more about us than we will ever understand — in this life.

In first John chapter 3, we can read of these wonderful promises of God's love towards us:

> 1. *Behold, what manner of love the Father hath*
> *bestowed upon us, that we should be called the*
> *sons of God: therefore the world knoweth us not,*
> *because it knew him not.*
> 2. *Beloved, now are we the sons of God, and*
> *it doth not yet appear what we shall be: but we*
> *know that, when he shall appear, we shall be like*
> *him; for we shall see him as he is.*

— 1 John 3:1–2

We become sons and daughters of the living God and when He returns again (not too far away) *"we shall be like him,"* and *"we shall see him as he is."*

The *"reject"* most certainly gives God all the praise and glory for having raised him up, out of the *"miry clay"* and he identifies with what the Psalmist had to say:

> 1. *I waited patiently for the LORD; and he inclined unto me, and heard my cry.*
> 2. *He brought me up also out of an horrible pit, out of the miry clay, and set my feet upon a rock, and established my goings.*
> 3. *And he hath put a new song in my mouth, even praise unto our God: many shall see it, and fear, and shall trust in the LORD.*
> 4. *Blessed is that man that maketh the LORD his trust, and respecteth not the proud, nor such as turn aside to lies.*
> 5. *Many, O LORD my God, are thy wonderful works which thou hast done, and thy thoughts which are to us-ward: they cannot be reckoned up in order unto thee: if I would declare and speak of them, they are more than can be numbered.*
> 6. *Sacrifice and offering thou didst not desire; mine ears hast thou opened: burnt offering and sin offering hast thou not required.*
> — Psalms 40:1–6

The time for burnt sacrifices and offerings is long over.

This verse in the book of Hebrews tells us we need to be offering up *"the fruit of our lips"*:

> 15. *By him therefore let us offer the sacrifice of*

praise to God continually, that is, the fruit of our lips giving thanks to his name.
— Hebrews 13:15

That is: *"giving thanks to his name."*

Now we can *"offer the sacrifice of praise to God continually."*

Instead of mumbling and grumbling about all that we perceive as wrong in the world these days — on both domestic and international fronts — rather, give praise and thanks to God for all that He is doing.

He is in the business of saving all who will heed His call.

Talk to your family and friends and neighbours — anyone who will hear.

Many of these will be as lost as was the *"reject."*

If you can identify with any of the feelings of rejection expressed within these pages — do not despair.

At his new church the *"reject"* developed his musical ability to the point where he was able to get together with others in a small band who would perform the gospel songs the *"reject"* managed to write.

Sixteen (16) of those songs got recorded over the years and got published through DistroKid™, in an attempt to reach out to others.

These can get streamed on digital music platforms such as: Amazon™, Apple Music™, Deezer™ (in France), Spotify™, YouTube™, and others.

The *"reject"* is not a great musician — yet he has enjoyed getting the opportunity to bring praises to God through the words and music he writes.

You could try searching for:

```
music by "Lawson Hanson"
```

Please include the quotation marks around his name to find his work because there are other bands and musicians called both "Lawson" and "Hanson" — none of whom is the one who resides in the *"reject's"* own skin.

In his retirement years the *"reject"* has spent his time writing a collection of small books — a bit like this one.

You can find these by searching for:

```
books by "Lawson Hanson"
```

Having made a complete turnaround, the *"reject"* has more or less made a resounding recovery.

Yes — as a youngster he may have been a complete loss. After decades of heavenly sent experience, with continual help and guidance from the God of Creation, perhaps now he is less of a loss than he once was.

Chapter 10

Reject gets new horizons

If we settle in our mind, as much as we are able, to live peaceably with everyone then we have probably outdone most.

Consider these sobering words from the book of James:

> 8. *If ye fulfil the royal law according to the scripture, Thou shalt love thy neighbour as thyself, ye do well:*
> 9. *But if ye have respect to persons, ye commit sin, and are convinced of the law as transgressors.*
> 10. *For whosoever shall keep the whole law, and yet offend in one point, he is guilty of all.*
> 11. *For he that said, Do not commit adultery, said also, Do not kill. Now if thou commit no adultery, yet if thou kill, thou art become a transgressor of the law.*
> 12. *So speak ye, and so do, as they that shall be judged by the law of liberty.*
> — James 2:8–12

If you have never read those verses before you might

consider these words recorded for us in the book of Deuteronomy from the time when God spoke with Moses and gave His instructions and commandments for us:

6. *I am the LORD thy God, which brought thee out of the land of Egypt, from the house of bondage.*
7. *Thou shalt have none other gods before me.*
8. *Thou shalt not make thee any graven image, or any likeness of any thing that is in heaven above, or that is in the earth beneath, or that is in the waters beneath the earth:*
9. *Thou shalt not bow down thyself unto them, nor serve them: for I the LORD thy God am a jealous God, visiting the iniquity of the fathers upon the children unto the third and fourth generation of them that hate me,*
10. *And shewing mercy unto thousands of them that love me and keep my commandments.*
11. *Thou shalt not take the name of the LORD thy God in vain: for the LORD will not hold him guiltless that taketh his name in vain.*
12. *Keep the sabbath day to sanctify it, as the LORD thy God hath commanded thee.*
13. *Six days thou shalt labour, and do all thy work:*
14. *But the seventh day is the sabbath of the LORD thy God: in it thou shalt not do any work, thou, nor thy son, nor thy daughter, nor thy manservant, nor thy maidservant, nor thine ox, nor thine ass, nor any of thy cattle, nor thy stranger that is within thy gates; that thy manservant and thy maidservant may rest as well as thou.*
15. *And remember that thou wast a servant in the land of Egypt, and that the LORD thy God brought thee out thence through a mighty hand*

*and by a stretched out arm: therefore the LORD
thy God commanded thee to keep the sabbath day.
16. Honour thy father and thy mother, as the
LORD thy God hath commanded thee; that thy
days may be prolonged, and that it may go well
with thee, in the land which the LORD thy God
giveth thee.
17. Thou shalt not kill.
18. Neither shalt thou commit adultery.
19. Neither shalt thou steal.
20. Neither shalt thou bear false witness against
thy neighbour.
21. Neither shalt thou desire thy neighbour's
wife, neither shalt thou covet thy neighbour's
house, his field, or his manservant, or his
maidservant, his ox, or his ass, or any thing that
is thy neighbour's.*
— Deuteronomy 5:6–21

We get reminded throughout the Bible, that our salvation
is not given because of anything that we do. Rather, it's
through the grace and mercy of God, and is made available
through the actions of Jesus Christ our Saviour:

> *5. Not by works of righteousness which we have
> done, but according to his mercy he saved us, by
> the washing of regeneration, and renewing of the
> Holy Ghost;
> 6. Which he shed on us abundantly through Jesus
> Christ our Saviour;
> 7. That being justified by his grace, we should be
> made heirs according to the hope of eternal life.*
> — Titus 3:5–7

Look again at that last verse. We get *"justified by His
grace"* and *"made heirs"* expecting to inherit *"the hope of
eternal life."*

Consider the reasons why we praise God.

He is Almighty God — the Creator of everything we can observe with all our God given senses and our own clever inventions.

He is the One True God. There's no other God who can answer our call.

He gave His own Son, Jesus Christ to be the perfect sacrifice for the sins of all humanity.

He has made a way for us to get reconciled to Him and have the opportunity to live together with God and Jesus and countless others throughout the rest of eternity.

It's difficult for us to comprehend the perfection of God and understand the reasons why God's own Son, Jesus Christ, needed to die in our place.

It has to do with the downfall of Adam whom God placed in the garden of Eden — a perfect paradise:

> 7. *And the LORD God formed man of the dust*
> *of the ground, and breathed into his nostrils the*
> *breath of life; and man became a living soul.*
> 8. *And the LORD God planted a garden eastward*
> *in Eden; and there he put the man whom he had*
> *formed.*
> 9. *And out of the ground made the LORD God*
> *to grow every tree that is pleasant to the sight,*
> *and good for food; the tree of life also in the*
> *midst of the garden, and the tree of knowledge*
> *of good and evil.*
> — Genesis 2:7–9

God created the human being with immense potential. God didn't want a robot that gets programmed to do what it does. God gave us the free will to choose to be more like Him. There was one non-negotiable instruction:

15. And the LORD God took the man, and put him into the garden of Eden to dress it and to keep it.
16. And the LORD God commanded the man, saying, Of every tree of the garden thou mayest freely eat:
17. But of the tree of the knowledge of good and evil, thou shalt not eat of it: for in the day that thou eatest thereof thou shalt surely die.
— Genesis 2:15–17

It seems Adam was unable to care about the veracity of God's commandment and as a result he fell from God's grace.

Jesus Christ came to repair the breach for all mankind.

Jesus got born into a human body and He knows how we feel:

14. Seeing then that we have a great high priest, that is passed into the heavens, Jesus the Son of God, let us hold fast our profession.
15. For we have not an high priest which cannot be touched with the feeling of our infirmities; but was in all points tempted like as we are, yet without sin.
16. Let us therefore come boldly unto the throne of grace, that we may obtain mercy, and find grace to help in time of need.
— Hebrews 4:14–16

Jesus knows how difficult we find it to stand up against the temptations of this earthly life.

In chapters 4 of the books of Matthew and Luke we can read of some of the temptation Jesus needed to withstand. Yet He did no sin.

These got followed by times of great anguish and torment at the time of His death by the hands of the religious experts of the day!

They had no idea. It seems their eyesight; their foresight; had gotten clouded. They could not see beyond their own maladjusted traditions.

The coming of John the Baptist and Jesus Christ had been foretold for centuries in the writings of their own prophets; like Joel and Malachi and others:

> 1. *Behold, I will send my messenger, and he shall prepare the way before me: and the LORD, whom ye seek, shall suddenly come to his temple, even the messenger of the covenant, whom ye delight in: behold, he shall come, saith the LORD of hosts.*
> — Malachi 3:1

We give great praise and thanks to Jesus Christ for enduring such torment and we give praises to God for enabling Him to carry that through.

All we need to do is be humble enough to accept God's gracious gift.

The entry requirements are not so onerous. *"Repent, and be baptized every one of you in the name of Jesus Christ for the remission of sins."*

Now we need to walk on in faith.

We need to safeguard against the endless deceptions of the world and its wily ways.

Jesus went to great lengths to illustrate how important is this matter, and showed how easy we can fall away from our faith if we will not take care.

I expect you could have heard of this parable He spoke:

5. *A sower went out to sow his seed: and as he sowed, some fell by the way side; and it was trodden down, and the fowls of the air devoured it.*
6. *And some fell upon a rock; and as soon as it was sprung up, it withered away, because it lacked moisture.*
7. *And some fell among thorns; and the thorns sprang up with it, and choked it.*
8. *And other fell on good ground, and sprang up, and bare fruit an hundredfold. And when he had said these things, he cried, He that hath ears to hear, let him hear.*
— Luke 8:5–8

Like us, the disciples of Jesus got perplexed by the meaning of His words and they asked Him for clarification.

Jesus answered them in this manner:

11. *Now the parable is this: The seed is the word of God.*
12. *Those by the way side are they that hear; then cometh the devil, and taketh away the word out of their hearts, lest they should believe and be saved.*
13. *They on the rock are they, which, when they hear, receive the word with joy; and these have no root, which for a while believe, and in time of temptation fall away.*
14. *And that which fell among thorns are they, which, when they have heard, go forth, and are choked with cares and riches and pleasures of this life, and bring no fruit to perfection.*
15. *But that on the good ground are they, which in an honest and good heart, having heard the word, keep it, and bring forth fruit with patience.*

— Luke 8:11–15

This means we need to get active in our relationship with God and ensure that none of the common cares and concerns of the world can steal us away from the wonderful experience God has bestowed on us.

We need to let the hardhearted and merciless thinking of this world get modified and replaced by God's wisdom.

The *"reject"* was a bit light on in that department. The Word of God has every contention covered:

> 5. *If any of you lack wisdom, let him ask of God, that giveth to all men liberally, and upbraideth not; and it shall be given him.*
> 6. *But let him ask in faith, nothing wavering. For he that wavereth is like a wave of the sea driven with the wind and tossed.*
> 7. *For let not that man think that he shall receive any thing of the Lord.*
> 8. *A double minded man is unstable in all his ways.*
> — James 1:5–8

We need to be single minded. Having made up our mind to follow the Lord, we need to remain steadfast. There is no need for continual variance.

If we will view our relationship with God as the most precious experience this world affords, then we can direct all our energy and focus on maintaining the relationship as we learn to speak with God every day.

The book of James contains more words of wisdom:

> 7. *Submit yourselves therefore to God. Resist the devil, and he will flee from you.*

8. Draw nigh to God, and he will draw nigh to
you. Cleanse your hands, ye sinners; and purify
your hearts, ye double minded.
10. Humble yourselves in the sight of the Lord,
and he shall lift you up.
— James 4:7–8, 10

Imagine and grasp hold of this!

We get to speak with the Creator of heaven and earth — on a one to One basis.

The born again reject is unable to imagine anything he would rather do.

Speaking freely with God is a priceless privilege.

We need to take care how we speak to God. If all we do is make a continual list of demands we think we need God to provide we could fall well short.

Again, James reminds us:

3. Ye ask, and receive not, because ye ask amiss,
that ye may consume it upon your lusts.
— James 4:3

Now that the *"reject"* has reached the age of seventy five years, it seems like there is still a bright future ahead.

He may not have a whole lot of years left in this current phase of life — who can tell?

One wonderful experience Jesus called *"the gift of the Father"* has given him hope for a far-ranging experience that extends into an everlasting future with God's family.

Please don't let the redemption of the *"reject"* be for no earthly good.

Put the same Bible given instructions to the test.

Call out to the God of the Bible in the way He has prescribed and let Him answer you in the specified manner.

The ability to speak in other (unlearned) tongues is the most gracious of gifts God could give us. In an instant in time we get to know He is real and that He cares for us in such a complete and loving way.

We get to converse with Him using our new language and we get to say everything we need to say in words we do not need to struggle to find in our own strength or inability.

Consider the promises contained in these beautiful verses from the book of Romans, chapter 8:

> 26. *Likewise the Spirit also helpeth our infirmities: for we know not what we should pray for as we ought: but the Spirit itself maketh intercession for us with groanings which cannot be uttered.*
> 27. *And he that searcheth the hearts knoweth what is the mind of the Spirit, because he maketh intercession for the saints according to the will of God.*
> 28. *And we know that all things work together for good to them that love God, to them who are the called according to his purpose.*
> — Romans 8:26–28

Consider these verses and the promises of God's provision:

> 8. *Will a man rob God? Yet ye have robbed me. But ye say, Wherein have we robbed thee? In tithes and offerings.*
> 9. *Ye are cursed with a curse: for ye have robbed me, even this whole nation.*

10. *Bring ye all the tithes into the storehouse,*
that there may be meat in mine house, and prove
me now herewith, saith the LORD of hosts, if
I will not open you the windows of heaven, and
pour you out a blessing, that there shall not be
room enough to receive it.
— Malachi 3:8–10

As soon as the *"reject"* had ceased smoking and drinking he discovered he had money left over each week to enable him to pay with ease a *"tithe"* for the work of God in small return for His boundless goodness towards him.

Our tithes help pay for communion elements (the bread and grape juice) and youth group activities and for upkeep and maintenance costs on our meeting place including expenses like energy and water rates.

Funds from our tithes also get sent to our overseas mission centres where there are Spirit-filled brothers and sisters in the Lord who stuggle to survive and thrive more than do we.

If we will do what God asks of us then He will be swift to open the windows of heaven and pour us out a blessing in return.

It's impossible to out-give God.

Don't ever skimp on giving back to God — of your time and your substance.

Support the meetings with your presence and involvement in tasks like handing out of the communion; helping with outreach activities and cleaning and other jobs that need to get done by somebody.

By the same author

Nonfiction

The Miracle Working God
Describes God's miracle working activity in the
previous 50 years of my life. — 2025.
ISBN 9781764057868 (EPUB)
ISBN 9781764057875 (paper book)

Love, Joy, Peace
Living a better life by the Grace of God. —
2025.
ISBN 9791764057844 (EPUB)
ISBN 9791764057851 (paper book)

Glory to God Everywhere You Are There
Describes the origins of my simple song of praise
from which I use its 3rd line for this title. —
2025.
ISBN 9781764057820 (EPUB)
ISBN 9781764057837 (paper book)

Jesus Says You Must Be Born Again
The most important information this world affords got given to us by Jesus Christ when He used those five imperative words. — 2025.
ISBN 9781764057813 (EPUB)
ISBN 9781764057806 (paper book)

Linux Clues
Tips and clues about using the Linux operating system from a seasoned Linux user. — 2025.
ISBN 9781764057882 (EPUB)
ISBN 9781764057899 (paper book)

9 dozen 9 character word puzzles
9 dozen 9 character word puzzles says it all; over 100 puzzles to enjoy. — 2025.
ISBN 9781764299701 (EPUB)
ISBN 9781764299718 (paper book)

Linux Bread Crumbs
Small morsels to help you learn to use the Linux operating system. — 2023.
ISBN 9798364005830 (paper book)

Paul's Question
Have you received the Holy Spirit? — 2023.
ISBN 9798857128381 (paper book)

To Day If You Will Hear His Voice
Encouragement to believe in God. — 2022.
ISBN 9798831130669 (paper book)

Fragments
Re-collected scattered writing fragments. — 2022.
ISBN 9798445585972 (paper book)

Take Another Look
If you have come across the full gospel message of Jesus Christ before and opted out — please take another look. — 2022.
ISBN 9798437605554 (paper book)

Song Lyrics
Notes and lyrics for 16 of my gospel songs with some links to help you listen to those. — 2022.
ISBN 9798434494120 (paper book)

The ramblings of an empty-headed fool
The title says everything you need to know about the author. — 2022.
ISBN 9798432196347 (paper book)

Fiction

The Ravenscroft Algorithm
Fictitious cyber security crime. — 2022.
ISBN 9798842106202 (paper book)

Broke Reef
Fictitious shipwreck on a West Australian Reef set in the late 19th century. — 2022.
ISBN 9798428316940 (paper book)

www.ingramcontent.com/pod-product-compliance
Lightning Source LLC
Chambersburg PA
CBHW071932020426
42331CB00010B/2829